i

Love Transcends

Divinely guided poetry from the heart

Dawn Warmack

A book of Love, Happiness, and Inspiration

Copyright © 2023

All Rights Reserved

ISBN: 979-8-9878123-9-6

Dedication

To all those who search for inspiration and Love

Acknowledgment

I would like to give sincere gratitude for all those who have inspired me throughout the years to follow my dreams with positivity and Love.

Contents

About the Author

Dawn Warmack is an American Poet. Born in a small town in Michigan, she always believed that staying positive was the key to success. She believes in following your dreams and trusting that by faith, anything is possible. That Love is the most powerful source in all things.

-GOD IS LOVE-

This book is written to be an Inspiration.

May all your dreams and hopes come true.

A note from the Author

A book of Love, Happiness, and Inspiration

Chapter 1: Inspirational Poems:

"Be Inspired, Love

Don't waste time.

Rush into what you want. "

Inspiration

"Remove the illusion.

Seek Truth,

Seek Clarity,

For then you will find healing,

And prosperity. **"**

Illusion

"Guiding Lights among us,

Prayers in silence,

A gift to the darkness,

To those in sadness and despair,

Seeking out the greater good.

For in that moment,

There is a peaceful calmness,

That rests in our hearts. "

Chosen

"So patiently we wait,

For the goodness In Devine Timing,

Our hearts and minds,

Rush towards the unknown.

Taking a leap of faith,

Knowing that happiness and truth lie in the unseen.

Patiently in the stillness

We wait. "

Devine Timing

"Push, Pull,

Back and forth,

Energy is constantly flowing.

The way you feel,

Steers the wheel,

To a destination unknowing. "

Energy

"Reach out,

Help,

Be different.

Forgive, Love,

Be different.

Be Generous,

Be courageous,

In all things,

Be different. "

Be Different

"How many shall fear the unknown,

Or believe it to be a curse?

And yet if we looked at it with opportunity,

We would see,

That fear is only the worst.

With happiness and love,

We open many doors,

It will be at that moment,

The unknown becomes visible.

In one accord. "

Unknown

"Courage is inner strength,

It is the power of control,

Sometimes courage is hard,

When we have an inner toll.

If we look to the greater good,

And pursue with a smile,

Courage becomes a form of love,

That's like an inner child. *"*

Courage

"When you reach for new beginnings,

It's not always easy.

One door closes,

Another opens.

We step out of our comfort zone.

We replace false ideas,

With new perspectives.

This new beginning

Becomes like home. "

New Beginnings

"Fast, forward, onward,

The messenger arrives,

Delivery of good news,

The sadness surely dies. "

Messenger

"*When all else fails,*

Smile.

When you're down,

Smile.

Think about all things you're blessed with

And know there is beauty inside you.

Your love can conquer all things.

If only you could smile. "

Smile

"If you've shattered into a million pieces,

And life has you down,

If you've lost everything in this world,

And nothing's turning around.

Remember to look into the sky,

You'll see help right there.

There's an angel holding on your arm,

To let you know they care. "

Broken Pieces

"You were born to make a difference,

Shine your light upon the world.

You were born with possibility,

With love and capability.

You were born to shine,

Now is the time.

Let the world see your light. "

Born

"*Change like the seasons,*

Like night into the day.

Sometimes the unknown scares us,

Sometimes we're scared to play.

If you have the courage,

To step into the light,

The change can be a great thing,

In which you take delight."

Change

"It takes power to break down barriers,

That some hold so tight.

It takes power to change the world,

From darkness into light.

We're all given power to make a difference,

If in that time we do.

The world can be a better place,

It's completely up to you. "

Power

"Don't delay your progress.

As you've worked so hard.

Don't delay your dreams,

As you've almost reached the stars.

Push beyond the path,

That some cannot see.

Remember why you started,

Continue to follow your dream. "

Don't Delay

"What stirs a light inside you?

What pushes you so far?

Its capabilities are beyond understanding.

When it matters of the heart.

So, feel that passion and drive,

Continue to succeed.

For in your success you reach,

You'll finally fill that dream. "

Motivation

"Everything around us is art.

The creative mind inside.

We see,

We feel,

This need is real,

To express the other side. "

Art

"Guided by a greater path,

We can finally see the light.

Moving from Negativity,

In what we know is right.

Carefully you take my hand,

And guide me along the way.

Your help is what guides me,

Through another day. "

Guidance

"Patiently we wait,

For the things we desire.

Wishing on a star,

Man, it seems so far.

Holding hope to the future,

We finally see.

Being patient is a Virtue,

And you have the key.

All you must do is turn it,

And walk on inside.

The answer is within you,

This you can't deny. "

Patience

"She sees beauty in the stars,

And everything she writes,

She sees perfection in the small things,

To her, it is life.

Joy is her abundance,

Kindness attributes to her soul.

Her lips speak of truth,

That's what makes her whole. "

Beauty

"When communication comes,

It's truly a delight.

It's only when your closed off,

That you keep everything inside.

If only you could trust,

You'd see I really care.

Pull down those walls,

You built so high,

I will be standing right there. "

Communication

"Be yourself and all you see,

Someone with integrity.

Open that door,

Give that smile.

Say "hello"

Once in a while. "

Be yourself.

"Heal your heart,

From within,

Let joy and happiness,

Settle in.

Let kindness touch,

Your inner soul.

Becoming who you need to be.

To become whole. "

Healing

"Wish fulfilled.

We manifest,

Each and every day.

Hopes and dreams.

Will come together.

In each and every way. "

Manifest

"*Look into your inner self,*

Creation at its core.

You'll find the perfect match for you,

All you need.

Is to open the door. "

Creative Self

"To help another,

To care for each other

Is there anything else to do?

When you give to those,

Who need it the most?

Your wishes will always come true."

Generosity

"Filled with excitement.

And adrenaline to,

Doing things I thought,

I'd never do.

Going for that goal,

Reaching for the sky.

This I know for sure,

My dreams won't pass me by. *"*

Adventurous

"Excitement in her eyes,

She rushes for the door.

Her dreams have finally come true,

To this she always swore.

There is no better feeling,

Then dreams that come true.

Her life is just beginning.

She is effortlessly brand new. "

Enthusiasm

"The love of the spirit

Transcends all around.

Working within us,

For true love to be found.

It guides our hearts,

And actions to.

Making life as we know it,

Completely brand new. "

Spirit

"It pushes us.

Past our comfort zones,

Making us dream big.

Into the unknown.

The light can't go out,

It shines right through.

The power inside us,

If we only knew. "

Vitality

"Be calm,

Be collective,

It's simple.

Help others,

Show integrity,

It's simple.

Be inspiring and uplifting,

It's simple.

Everything you put your mind to,

Is simple. "

Simple

"The heart is pure.

From within,

The emotions you feel,

Start to begin.

Craving love,

Craving Insight.

The dreams you have,

Start to ignite. "

Sensitive

"Let go of the past,

It holds you down.

Let go of fear,

From all around.

Pursue your dreams,

Don't let go.

For if you do,

You'll never know.

You'll never know,

If that wish you had,

Will come again,

So just be glad. "

Release

"The smell of the book,

She holds in her hand,

The sounds of the pages turning.

The taste of wine,

She sips while she reads,

There's nothing more.

She's yearning. "

Exquisite

"*It can inspire you,*

Or excite you,

Push you closer to your dreams.

It can make you fall in love,

Or take it to extremes.

Whatever the occasion,

Music is always there.

To listen and inspire,

In this world we share. "

Music

"Family Laughter,

Hugs so tight.

Sitting at the table,

Our blessings in sight.

The laughter,

The talks,

The wishes are true.

Blessings that mean the most,

Are sitting next to you. "

Blessings

"We ask for miracles,

But can we believe?

For those without faith,

Cannot achieve.

To think in the light,

And not in the dark,

A miracle will happen,

Just believe in your heart. "

Miracle

"The pouring of blessings,

The energy arrives,

The windfall of your dreams,

Is now on your side.

Hold on to your hope,

Dreams do come true.

This windfall of blessings,

Was meant for you. "

Windfall

"They say you're unrecognizable,

The changes you've gone through.

But maybe that's a good thing,

You've reached a better you.

You smile more often now,

And laugh now to.

You've finally reached a place,

To be a better you. **"**

Unrecognizable

"Why do you contemplate inside your mind?

If you know what's right?

Follow your intuition,

It's your guiding light."

Contemplate

"There are simple pleasures in happiness,

And smiling all the time.

There's goodness in our hearts,

We feel the need to shine.

When that joy comes over you,

Give it to those who see.

The light that's inside of you,

You cannot let it be. "

Joy

"We come together in harmony,

For all of humanity.

Working towards the greater good,

Helping each other,

Just like we should. "

Harmony

"They watch us while we sleep,

Into the early morn,

They put us on a straight path,

When everything else is torn.

The goodness they provide,

One can truly see,

God has a perfect angel,

Watching over me. "

Angels

"That feeling that you get,

When you hear a funny joke,

When it hurts so much inside,

You almost start to choke.

This is my excitement,

The way I love to be,

Laughing so much it hurts,

When you're right next to me. "

Laughing

"Balance your mind,

Calm your heart,

Even when,

You're worlds apart.

Rest, Relax,

Rejuvenate to.

All to make,

A better you. "

Refresh

"Don't be afraid, Imagine.

Close your eyes and see the light.

Everything is possible,

With endlessness in sight. "

Imagine

"Reach for the stars,

Reach for the sky,

Change the way you think,

Without asking why.

Believe in yourself,

Because when you do,

That's when your dreams,

Start coming true. "

Change

"*The smell of coffee brewing,*

The children running around.

The laughter of the family,

You can't forget the sound.

Home is where the heart is,

That's what they've always said.

Home is where I love,

Snuggled in my bed. "

Home

"*Bring to life the spirit within,*

Awaken our hearts,

So, we can begin.

Begin on this journey,

So, we can see,

The awakening beauty,

Inside of me.

Awakening

"Be the light,

That shines in the darkness,

That opens many hearts.

For if you do,

The light shines through,

And darkness will depart. ,,

The light

Chapter 2: Love Poems:

"Love is Timeless,

It reaches places further than the eye can see.

It grabs hold of your heart,

The place where it starts.

To this you can guarantee. "

Timeless

"Guided by love,

We found each other.

In the realm of possibility.

Seeking only love,

Holding a connection to the divine,

Separated by what we call "life."

For a short period of time.

To reconnect once again.

And shine our light on the world. "

Earth Angels

"You have the key,

It's in your hands.

My heart is aware of who you are.

Come closer and let me see your energy,

Let me feel the connection,

Turn the key."

Open My Heart

"A skipped heartbeat,

A deep breath,

The eyes of an angel,

I can't forget.

It's as though,

God himself brought you here,

Transcending Love,

I do not fear. "

Love Transcends

"Together as one,

They trust each other.

Guided by pure love,

They lean on each other's strengths.

Forgiving, Forgetting, and moving forward,

They make a promise to love forever. "

Courtship

"There are many stars in the sky,

But none shine as bright as you.

Your energy,

Your pureness.

It captivates the very essence of the galaxy.

By far the most beautiful

Light in the universe. "

The Star

"Love cannot be hidden,

It finds ways to come out.

Through the holes

Of a broken soul

It heals and mends.

The heart. "

Hidden

"Clarify for me Dear God

That this love does exist.

In our hearts we have hope in you.

In the unseen love,

Our wishes come true.

Clarify for me Dear God

Let me take that leap.

For the hope that has been revealed,

In my heart I will keep. "

Clarify

"Gentle sentiments

Soft whispers abound.

Transcending Love

All around.

Wishes sent to the sky.

With hope nearby.

To have this love, flourish. "

Flourish

"Cherish the time we have.

The people that you love,

Cherish the many blessings.

We get from Heaven up above.

For in all you do,

The truth will be shown.

To this greater crowd,

Your heart will be made known. "

Cherish

"They run; they play.

They look up to you.

Their little hearts

See all you do.

The need to see,

Your loving care,

They need to know,

You'll always be there. "

Little Hearts

"Open your heart,

Feel the love.

Open your eyes,

See the love.

In all things,

Be love. "

Feel the Love

"She sees beauty in candlelight dinners.

And simple pleasures.

The reflection of the light.

She sees happiness.

In a gentle smile

And passion in his eyes.

She sees joy in all things,

Big and small,

Love tried and true.

But the perfection of a candlelight dinner,

This will surely do. "

Candlelight

"She cherishes love,

More than anything else.

Within her she feels,

The desire to give and help others,

To her, it's so unreal.

There is no understanding,

To this concept that she shows,

She does it because she loves,

Even when no one knows. "

Love

"Todays the day,

I should receive,

A letter from a person that means most to me.

I wait by the window,

With excitement inside.

Almost that time,

For my letter to arrive. "

The Letter

"Your presence lights up the me,

I never knew existed.

Your smile lights up my heart.

If only in another world,

We wouldn't be apart.

So, until that day,

I'll sit and pray,

For a miracle to come.

And think about the life I can have,

When you are the one. "

Light up my world

"Do you remember what it feels like?

To be crazy in love?

To feel that happiness

Rush over you,

You just can't get enough.

Just the thought of being in love,

Head over heels.

To keep that feeling going

To keep turning that wheel.

To be crazy in love,

Now that, is something real. "

Crazy in Love

"Take off the mask,

To reveal

The true feelings you hide inside.

I'm a reader of hearts you see,

That cannot work on me.

I know your heart is good,

So come out from behind the mask.

All I want to do is love you,

You don't even have to ask. "

Lift the mask.

"She's the queen of her kingdom,

She holds her head up high.

Nothing can get passed her,

Especially a lie.

She appreciates kindness and love,

And thoughtful little gifts.

She's waiting for her prince charming.

For that one,

True loves kiss. "

The Queen

"He put forever in their hearts,

To never guess a day.

He followed it with perfect love,

That never goes away."

Forever

"Thoughts of you

Throughout the day.

Playing my favorite song.

My heart skips a beat,

When we meet,

The synchronicity is strong. "

Synchronicity

"*It must be beautiful to be in your heart,*

To feel the love of such a soul.

The pureness of your intentions

Means more to me then gold.

The way you shower me with love,

And help in every way.

The way you think of me in your heart.

Each and every day.

To find something as pure as this,

My heart feels so full.

Nothing will ever take you away.

You mean more to me then gold."

In your heart

"The scales have balanced,

Oh, so true.

When there's me,

There's also you.

Love like ours

Is hard to find.

Holding forever,

Until the end of time. "

Justice

"Your existence is perfect,

Everything about you is Devine.

When I look into your eyes,

I see the end of time.

I cherish the moments I have you,

Each and every day.

You'll always be perfect for me,

In each and every way. "

Perfect

"He goes beyond himself,

To give roses and cards.

To say, "I love you".

He disregards the opinions of others.

And loves with all his heart.

To him you're more than a wish.

More than something that came true.

You're the one of his dreams,

No one else will do. "

Thoughtful

"Those eyes,

Those lips,

That smile,

Can you ask for more?

You're simply adorable,

My heart drops to the floor.

If I could pick it up,

I wouldn't touch a thing.

You're simply adorable,

My heart can't help but sing. "

Adorable

"He was her beloved,

Passion from the start.

She loved everything about him,

Especially his heart.

Within her hands she trusted,

To give him loving care.

To give them a life of love,

Forever they would share. "

Beloved

"Complete and utter devotion,

To the love they know.

Growing old together,

They're willing to undergo.

Lifting each other up,

Cherishing their love.

Something so very precious,

Sent from Heaven up above. "

Devotion

"Pure Love,

True care,

The Love from God,

I'll always share.

The one and only

Agape Love,

Sent to us.

From heaven above. "

Agape Love

"My soul calls out to you,

But can you hear?

The distance between us,

Is far too clear.

In the depths of my heart,

I yearn for your love.

I know it's truly,

Sent from above. "

Yearning

"From that moment you arrived,

You captivated my heart.

I knew from the moment,

We would never be apart.

The way you look at me,

And smile with delight.

I thank God for you,

Both day and night. "

A Mothers love

"The sweetness of your love,

The gentleness of your touch.

The way you look into my eyes,

I just cannot get enough.

If this love is for real,

I would have to believe.

I'm walking into heaven,

Falling on my knees. "

Honey

Chapter 3: Nature Poems:

"A bird never looks beneath her wings,

She trusts in the wind to lift her up,

She flies to the heavens,

In belief,

That, what is here,

Is enough. "

Beneath her wings

"Fiercely Hot

Or Lukewarm,

How the sun makes me smile.

With a cool breeze,

I feel at ease,

And joyfully at peace. "

The Sun

"The crow is thought to be,

A reflection of a bad enemy.

But I see beauty,

In its wings,

The power in its intelligence.

The softness in its heart. "

The Crow

"Planting seeds of love

Coming up through the soil,

This planted love seed sprouts,

Making its way out.

Cherished by the sun,

And blessed by the rain,

This love will truly blossom,

Time and time again."

Garden

"Light in the dark,

The moon shines so bright,

Peering through the clouds,

The most beautiful thing in sight.

Left untouched and perfect,

I look into the sky,

Blessed by such a simple thing,

In the darkening of the night."

The Moon

"Let it rain on your shoulders,

Let it drop from your hair,

Let it touch the very skin.

God blessed you with,

Look up into the air.

Dance around like a small child,

Singing in the storm,

Let the floodgates of heaven open,

Until the early morn. "

Let it rain.

"The warm summer breeze,

The crickets in the night.

The splashing of the water,

Is perfectly in sight.

This is what I desire,

On a summer's day,

Praying that the summer,

Will be here to stay. "

Warm Breeze

"All the colors

That you can see.

The sky is beautiful,

How can it be?

Another world,

Or so it seems.

It's almost like heaven.

Is looking down on me.

To shine its colors.

And all its glory,

Will someday tell,

A beautiful story. "

The Rainbow

"*With strength and honor,*

The trees grow tall.

It's magnificent beauty.

Surrounds us all.

Many lifetimes

Could pass us by

All the while,

It will touch the sky. "

The Tree

"Quietly at peace,

We stand still.

Listening to the calmness of the night.

The beauty of nature,

The smell of the rain.

The sound of the wind,

Stand still,

And let it in. "

Stand Still

"Looking into the field

She sees flowers,

Floating in the breeze.

She smells the sweet scent of perfection,

The beauty of the trees.

The sun going down,

The crickets in the night.

The beauty of nature,

Is plain in sight."

Flowers

DAWN WARMACK

You can conquer the
world with love....

www.ingramcontent.com/pod-product-compliance
Lightning Source LLC
LaVergne TN
LVHW052034080426
835513LV00018B/2314